Air Fryer

Cookbook

2021

Make mouthwatering
and delicious recipes
with your amazing air fryer
and keep on
enjoying healthy meals

SAMANTHA FIELD

Contents

Introduction

For a majority of people, fried foods act like a guilty pleasure. They're soft on the inside and crunchy on the outside. Is there anything about fried foods that you don't like? Without any doubt, there's the issue of the extra oil used to cook them, which is unhealthy. So, what are your choices if you want fried foods but don't like the unhealthy way they're prepared? You can always scale down and limit the intake. Is there anything else that you can do? It should come as no surprise that you can get the deep-fried flavor by avoiding the unhealthy amount of cooking oil by using air fryers. Deep fryers could be used to cook a wide range of foods. They can be used to produce anything from snacks like French fries to bigger dishes such as chicken pieces. Some deep fryers are large enough to cook a whole turkey. They work by rapidly cooking food in extremely hot oil. The food is normally put in a basket and then dipped into the hot oil. The hot oil conducts heat very well, and also, because the food is immersed, it cooks evenly on both sides. Since you don't have to bake one side at a time, this cuts down on cooking time compared to pan-frying. The Maillard effect occurs when foods are deep-fried. This is a response that turns foods golden brown by breaking down the proteins and sugars on their surface. Deep frying also eliminates all of the water from the food's outer layer, leaving it dry and locking in the moisture. There is a plethora of kitchen equipment that is available online. Electric pressure cookers, deep fryers, air fryers, and other appliances are all different kinds of kitchen equipment that can be bought from the market and are affordable. In air frying, the air is blown down into a heating element by a fan on the fryer. The food is put in a basket identical to that of a deep fryer, and air flows through and around it. The air in the air fryer bounces off the bottom and backs up the food. The hot air heats the food on both sides while also causing the Maillard reaction, which results in a crispy outer crust. However, Air Fryers take a special position among them all because they are the only system that is safe. In reality, this is the only device on the market that allows you to cook without or with very little oil. The food is cooked in an air fryer using super-heated air. Thanks to their lower fat and calorie content, air-fried foods are a better substitute for deep-fried foods. Instead of fully soaking the food in oil, air-frying uses just a tablespoon of oil to create a flavor and texture that is equivalent to deep-fried foods.

CHAPTER 1: Air Frying and its Advantages

An Air Fryer is an appliance that cooks food with very little to no oil. This makes it a popular item for many people because it makes frying healthier. No one might imagine that frying had just gotten better when this product first came out. Air fryers can cook with very little oil, if not none at all. Some versions are unable to do so without the use of oil, although others are capable of doing so. Even if it is capable of doing that, the flavor is remarkably different, so most people use a small amount of oil instead. After all, how much would you give up on taste for the sake of health? All the air fryers come with a basket. The air fryer's basket is the container inside the unit where you place your food for frying. Since the basket is normally the one containing the food, the size of the basket decides the amount of food that can be cooked in your Air Fryer. To put it another way, a big basket will cook more food than a small and/or medium basket. Air fried food has a distinct flavor from normal fried food. Regular fried food is fried in a large amount of oil, which gives it a distinct taste. However, you must not get discouraged by the said. Both have distinct flavors, though some people enjoy the taste of Air Fried food over that of Deep-Fried food. So, if you haven't done it yet, it's certainly worth a try. Let's take a look at how deep fryers and air fryers function first.

1.1 Deep frying and Air frying

- Deep fryers necessarily require a decent amount of oil to properly submerge the food. Foods cooked in an air fryer can be cooked with as little as a tablespoon of oil or even no oil at all.

- Because deep-frying oil penetrates the food deeper, food fried in a deep fryer typically has a thicker and crispier crust. • Whereas air fryers use little or no oil, certain foods can come out dryer than those cooked in a deep fryer.

- Deep fryers are only used for frying foods. You may use an air fryer with a variety of cooking techniques, including grilling. You may also use an air flyer for baking desserts.

- Since air fryers use very little or no oil, they are much easier to clean than deep fryers. It may also be inconvenient to dispose of huge quantities of cooking oil.

1.2 Is Cooking with an Air Fryer Healthy?

Air frying is a common kitchen appliance since it is considered a safe, guilt-free way to consume your preferred fried foods. Famous foods such as French fries, empanadas, chicken wings and fish sticks are said to contain less fat. A common kitchen device for frying foods like beef, pastries and potato chips is an air fryer. It provides a crunchy and crispy exterior by circulating hot air all around food. This also triggers the Maillard reaction, which happens when an amino acid along with reducing sugar comes into contact with each other in the presence of heat. Foods alter their color and taste as a result of it. Because of their reduced fat and calorie content, most people perceive air-fried foods to be a healthier alternative to deep-fried foods. Instead of fully submerging the food in oil, air-frying uses just a tablespoon to create a flavor and feel that is comparable to deep-fried foods. Since they need less oil to achieve a comparable flavor, air-fried foods are thought to be better than deep-fried foods.

Using an air fryer can help cut the fat content

Foods prepared by deep-frying have a higher fat content than foods prepared by other methods. A fried chicken breast, for example, contains more fat than roasted chicken of the same size. Some of the air fryer producing companies say that using an air fryer will minimize the fat content of fried foods by up to 75%. This is due to the fact that air fryers use a lot less fat than conventional deep fryers. Many deep-fried recipes call for up to three cups (seven hundred fifty ml) of oil, but air-fried foods do need around 1 tablespoon (15 ml). Deep fryers use approximately fifty times more oil as compared to air fryers, and although the food does not consume any of that oil, using an air fryer will greatly reduce the food's total fat content. When researchers measured the properties of deep-fried with air-fried French fries, they discovered that air-frying created a product with slightly less fat but the comparable color & moisture content. This may have a big effect on your health, as consuming more fat from vegetable oils has been related to an elevated risk of heart disease and inflammation.

Switching to an air fryer may aid in weight loss

Deep-fried foods are rich in fat, and they're still high in calories, which can lead to weight gain. A sample of 33,542 Spanish adults discovered that eating more fried foods was linked to a higher risk of obesity. Swapping deep-fried foods for air-fried foods might be a smart way to start if you're trying to lose weight. Dietary fat contains more than twice as many calories/gram as other macro nutrients such as protein and carbohydrates, with 9 calories per gram. Moving to an air fryer can be a simple way to reduce calories and help you control your weight because air-fried foods have less fat than deep-fried foods. Air-fried foods contain less fat than deep-fried foods, which can help you minimize calories and sustain a healthier weight.

Air fryers can decrease the formation of harmful compounds

Frying food can produce potentially harmful compounds like acrylamide, in addition to being higher in fat and calories. Acrylamide is a carbohydrate-rich food compound produced under high-heat cooking methods such as frying. Acrylamide is listed as a "probable human carcinogen" by the International Agency for Research on Cancer, which means that some research suggests it may be related to cancer growth. Acrylamide is also suspected to be carcinogenic to humans, according to the Environmental Protection Agency. Using an air fryer instead of a deep fryer will help reduce the amount of acrylamide in your fried foods. In fact, when compared to conventional deep-frying, one study showed that air-frying lowered acrylamide by up to 90%. However, it's crucial to keep in mind that other potentially dangerous compounds can develop during the air-frying process. Other potentially harmful chemicals produced by high-heat cooking include aldehydes, heterocyclic amines, and polycyclic aromatic hydrocarbons, which have been related to an elevated risk

of cancer. To find out how air-frying influences the production of these substances, further research is required. Using an air fryer, on the other hand, will decrease the amount of sugar, calories, and potentially unhealthy compounds in the food as opposed to deep-frying.

Cook Multiple Dishes

With an air fryer, you can cook several dishes at once, saving a lot of time. This is similar to having a skillet, deep fryer, toaster, and microwave together in one system. You can also make a range of nutritious dishes with it, such as air fryer salmon dishes. Salmon is known for its many health benefits, and now that you have an air fryer, you won't have any trouble frying it. Air Fryer Chocolate Chip Cookies, Crispy Air Fryer Bacon, Crispy Air Fryer Baked Potatoes, Air Fryer Mozzarella Sticks and Air Fryer Buttermilk Fried Chicken are only a few of the other recipes you can try.

It is Safe

Deep frying has a number of drawbacks, one of which being the possibility of hot oil spills or the constant splashing of oil while frying. You don't have to be concerned about this for air fryers, so there's no chance of leaking or splashing oil. You still won't have to be concerned with your children being in the kitchen. You won't have to think about overheating or burnt food because it has an auto-shut option that activates once the cooking is done. When opposed to the conventional deep-frying process, air fryers have higher safety standards.

1.3 Air Fryer vs. Deep Fryer

Now that you have a clear understanding of how each of these devices works, the next question is which one is the better option.

Taste

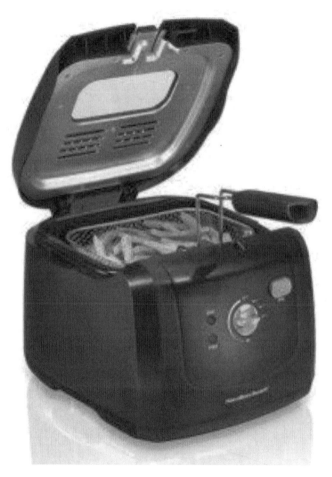

If the taste of fried foods is your top priority, a deep fryer is a way to go. While air fryers can produce a crispy exterior comparable to that of a deep fryer, nothing compares to the consistency of real deep-fried food. Additionally, some foods can come out drier in an air fryer than they would in a deep fryer. In terms of flavor, the deep fryer is unquestionably the winner.

Health

When it comes to deep-fried foods, the primary worry is normally health. There is an abundance of fat applied to the foods when they are entirely immersed in a kind

of cooking oil. You don't require much oil for an air fryer, or you can use a fraction of the oil you will usually need, decreasing the fat content of the meal. The air fryer takes the first spot in this segment when it comes to health.

Versatility

An air fryer is a good choice if you'd like an appliance that will do more than just frying food. Accessories for grilling and roasting items are available in stores. An air fryer can also be used to prepare desserts. If you're looking for a device that's exclusively for deep frying and want the crispy deep-fried finish, a deep fryer is a way to go.

1.4 Air frying health pros and cons

Thanks to modern cooking technology that needs less oil, less time to fry, plus other culinary equipment on your table, air frying has become a common cooking technique. You may choose to use this method instead of shallow frying, which is when food is cooked in a skillet with just a little oil or fat, or deep-frying, which is when food is cooked in a skillet with a lot of fat or oil. You might also think of the following pros and cons:

Pros of air fryers

They are efficient in terms of energy.

They use less oil and consume low energy than a traditional oven. Air-fried foods contain 70-80% fewer calories than deep-fried foods, and the fat drains from the item during frying.

They also save time and resources because they don't need many hot oils that can splatter.

Cons of air fryers

Keep an eye on the food because it cooks quickly at 300 to 400 degrees. If the food is cooked for some minutes more, then you've got burnt food, a known cause of cancer.

Also, foods with less fat and greater boiling temperatures will dry out easily, so if you want to cook with more than a few people, you'll have to do so in sections.

Because BPA is a carcinogen, be sure the fryer you buy is made up of BPA-free plastic.

The types of food you may prepare are rather minimal. Chicken and Potatoes are the most common.

1.5 Selecting the Best Air Fryer

Of course, you're still curious about what points you need to focus on. When it comes to choosing a model, there are a few important considerations to bear in mind. These can be outlined and defined in the following way:

Capacity

First and foremost, you must define the capacity. You must choose a model that can cook the amount of food you want. Selecting a model that is too big will result in waste while selecting a model that is too small will cause you to prepare the same thing in quantities.

Functionality and Versatility

Of course, an air fryer is required by your need in order to accomplish your objectives. It's needless to spend money on anything that won't meet your needs. So, keep the requirements in mind and purchase anything that will meet them.

Price

Affordability is, of course, extremely necessary. You must keep this in mind and check out the one that is the perfect match for your budget.

Safety

Another important factor is to consider a model's safety. The level of safety offered by a model is important for both you as well as your device. Yes, despite the fact that all businesses strive to keep all models safe, it is also something to be aware of. This is because one of the things you can never consider risking is your

wellbeing.

The opinion of people who have already used it

People who have used a model before are more knowledgeable about it than you are. And therefore, of course, paying attention to them is important. So, we've based our ultimate evaluation on what a lot of people who have used it have to say, and we're hoping that they'll be able to educate us so that we can make better decisions possible. We would, of course, learn from their experience.

Conclusion

The right one for you may not necessarily be the best one available. The best one for you is decided by the unique criteria. The best model for you is one that meets all of the requirements at a fair price. As a consequence, you must keep your eyes as well as ears open and perform analysis. After that, you would go out and purchase the one that is right for you and meets the requirements.

1.6 Evidence on Air Fryers as a really healthy way of cooking your food

Air fryers are thought to be a simple way to make some of your favorite, less-than-healthy meals (fried chicken and golden French fries) much nutritious and healthier without losing flavor. However, we have to find the evidence to prove this claim. Is it true that air fryers are healthy? Here's a look at how these hot new kitchen appliances operate, whether air frying is genuinely a better option than deep-frying and whether air fryers are truly safe to use on a daily basis.

The Claim

Air frying food is a safe and healthy option over deep-frying.

The Evidence

With a fraction of the oil used as compared to deep-frying, air fryers may give food a crispy as well as a crunchy texture. Since deep fryers use liquid fat to pass heat to food, this is possible. Air fryers, on the other hand, use convection heating, in which hot air is circulated quickly, and tiny oil droplets are sprayed around the product. The hot air movement and 360-degree exposure to the food produce a dry, browned crust that resembles deep-frying. Because of the convection process, air fryers only use a tablespoon or two of oil to achieve a fried-like texture. Since you don't need more oil to start with, air-fried foods consume far less fat than deep-fried foods. Numerous tablespoons to a half cup of oil are needed even for pan-frying. And, in general, more fat means more calories.

Case in point

A deep-fried chicken thigh contains about two hundred and fifty calories and nineteen grams of fat. A fried one, on the other hand, has just one hundred and thirty-five calories and five grams of fat. While this does not sound like much, if you eat a lot of deep-fried foods, it will add up to an elevated chance of obesity and weight gain over time. Air frying can also be a safe way to reduce trans fats, which are a form of refined fat linked to heart disease as well as type 2 diabetes. Many restaurants use trans-fat-containing vegetable oils like soybean or canola to deep-fry their food. Reusing frying oil, whether in a restaurant or at home, has been found to increase blood pressure, cholesterol, and inflammation in the arteries. There's even the matter of carcinogens to consider. Air frying has been found to create considerably fewer acrylamides; toxic compounds formed when the amino acids in foods like potatoes and/or bread are heated to extremely high temperatures. However, when it comes to cooking meat, high temperatures from both methods have the potential to produce polycyclic aromatic hydrocarbons (PAHs) as well as heterocyclic amines (HCAs), particularly if the meat is burnt. According to the National Cancer Institute, both of these chemicals can increase the risk of cancer.

The Verdict

Air-fried foods have fewer calories and fat than deep-fried foods, which could be healthier for the waistline over time. But that's just the start. Air frying will help you prevent trans fats while still protecting your heart. It will also help you avoid toxic chemicals called acrylamides that have been linked to cancer

CHAPTER 2: Air Fryer Breakfast Recipes

This chapter contains a collection of tasty breakfast recipes that you can easily make in the air fryer.

2.1 Air-Fryer Apple Fritters

Preparation time

18 minutes

Servings

15 persons

Nutritional facts

145 calories per one fritter

Ingredients

We have listed below the ingredients that would be required by you for cooking this healthy and tasty meal on your home air fryer:

- Cooking spray
- One and a half cup all-purpose flour

- A quarter cup of sugar

- Two teaspoons baking powder

- One and a half teaspoon ground cinnamon

- Half teaspoon salt

- Two-third cup milk

- Two large eggs, room temperature

- One tablespoon lemon juice

- One and a half teaspoon vanilla extract, divided

- Two medium Honey crisp apples, peeled and chopped

- A quarter cup butter

- One cup confectioners' sugar

- One tablespoon 2% milk

Instructions

- Given below are the detailed instructions for cooking this tasty meal on your air fryer. You need to follow these instructions in the given order.

- Spray the air-fryer basket with cooking spray and line it with parchment paper (cut to fit). Preheat the air fryer to four hundred ten degrees Fahrenheit.

- Mix sugar, flour, baking powder, cinnamon, and salt in a large mixing bowl. Combine the eggs, milk, lemon juice and one tsp vanilla extract in a mixing bowl and swirl just until combined. Apples should be folded in.

- Drop dough by one-fourth cupfuls 2-in. apart into an air-fryer basket in batches. Using cooking oil, spritz the surface. Cook for 5-6 minutes until it's golden brown. Continue to air-fry fritters till golden brown, around 1-2 minutes.

- In a shallow saucepan, melt the butter over medium-high heat. Cook, sometimes stirring, until the butter begins to brown & foam, about 5 minutes. Remove from the heat and allow it to cool slightly. Toss the browned butter with the confectioners' sugar, one tablespoon milk, and the remaining half tsp vanilla extract; whisk until smooth. Before serving, drizzle the over the fritters.

2.2 Air-Fryer Peppermint Lava Cakes

Preparation time

30 minutes

Servings

4 persons

Nutritional facts

563 calories

Ingredients

We have listed below the ingredients that would be required by you for cooking this healthy and tasty meal on your home air fryer:

- Two egg yolks, room temperature

- Two eggs, room temperature

- 6 tbsp flour

- One tsp peppermint extract

- 2/3 cup semisweet chocolate chips

- A half-cup butter, cubed

- One cup confectioners' sugar

- Two tbsp peppermint candies, finely crushed, optional

Instructions

Given below are the detailed instructions for cooking this tasty meal on your air fryer. You need to follow these instructions in the given order.

- Heat air fryer to 375° F.

- Melt butter and chocolate chips in a microwave-safe bowl for 30 seconds, stirring until smooth. Combine confectioners' sugar, whites, egg yolks and extract in a mixing bowl and whisk until smooth. Fold in the flour.

- Grease & flour four 4-ounce ramekins and then spill batter into them. Must not overfill the bottle. Place ramekins on a tray in the air-fryer basket and cook for 10-12 minutes, till the thermometer gives a reading of 160° and the edges of the cakes are set. Don't overcook.

- Remove from the basket and set aside for 5 minutes. To remove the cake, gently loop a knife along the edges of the ramekins several times. Then invert onto the dessert plates. Crushed candies should be sprinkled on top.

- Serve right away.

2.3 Air-Fryer Chocolate Chip Oatmeal Cookies

Preparation time

30 minutes

Servings

6 dozen

Nutritional facts

102 calories per one cookie

Ingredients

We have listed below the ingredients that would be required by you for cooking this healthy and tasty meal on your home air fryer:

- 3/4 cup packed brown sugar
- 2 large eggs, room temperature
- One teaspoon vanilla extract
- 3 cups quick-cooking oats
- One and a half cup all-purpose flour
- One package (3.4 ounces) instant vanilla pudding mix
- One teaspoon baking soda
- One teaspoon salt
- Two cups semisweet chocolate chips
- One cup butter softened
- 3/4 cup sugar
- One cup chopped nuts

Instructions

- Given below are the detailed instructions for cooking this tasty meal on your air fryer. You need to follow these instructions in the given order.
- Heat air fryer to 325° F.
- Cream sugar and butter in a large mixing bowl till light and fluffy, around 5-7 minutes. In a separate bowl, whisk together the eggs as well as vanilla extract.

Whisk together the flour, oats, baking soda, dry pudding mix and salt in a small bowl; slowly beat into the creamed mixture. Mix the chocolate chips and nuts.

- Drop tablespoonfuls of dough onto baking sheets and flatten gently. Place 1 inch apart on a greased tray in an air-fryer basket in batches. Cook for 8-10 minutes until it is lightly browned. Allow it to cool on wire racks.

2.4 Air-Fryer Lime Macaroons

Preparation time

25 minutes

Servings

30 cookies

Nutritional facts

133 calories per one cookie

Ingredients

We have listed below the ingredients that would be required by you for cooking this healthy and tasty meal on your home air fryer:

- One and a half teaspoon grated lime zest
- A one-fourth teaspoon of salt
- A one fourth teaspoon almond extract
- 1 package (14 ounces) sweetened shredded coconut
- Four large egg whites, room temperature
- 2/3 cup sugar
- Three tablespoons gin
- A half-cup all-purpose flour
- 8 ounces white baking chocolate, melted

Instructions

Given below are the detailed instructions for cooking this tasty meal on your air fryer. You need to follow these instructions in the given order.

- Heat air fryer to 350° F.
- Whisk together the 1st 6 ingredients till well mixed. Toss the coconut with the flour in a separate dish, and then insert the egg white mixture.
- Place by tablespoonfuls one inch apart on a greased tray in the air-fryer basket in batches. Cook for 4-5 minutes, or till browned. Let it cool on wire racks.
- Dip the bottoms of the macarons into the molten chocolate and let the excess

run off. Put on the waxed paper and set aside to dry. These can easily be stored in an airtight container.

2.5 Crispy Air Fryer Breakfast Burritos

Preparation time

50 minutes

Servings

8 burritos

Nutritional facts

240 calories

Ingredients

We have listed below the ingredients that would be required by you for cooking this healthy and tasty meal on your home air fryer:

Ingredients for the potatoes

- One tablespoon arrowroot powder/starch (optional for crisp)
- Two teaspoons paprika
- One teaspoon garlic powder
- A half teaspoon onion powder
- One-pound Yukon gold potatoes or russet, sliced into half-inch cubes (3–4, 2 large, small potatoes)
- 2 tablespoons avocado oil
- One teaspoon salt
- A half teaspoon of black pepper

Ingredients for the ground sausage

- One-pound breakfast pork, seasoned and ground
- One (four-ounce) can of green chilies, diced

Ingredients for the scrambled eggs

- Eight eggs whisked
- Two tbsp. milk
- A half tsp. salt & pepper

Ingredients for the burritos

- Approx. 1 cup cheddar cheese

- Seven to eight burrito size tortillas (10 inch)

- hot sauce, sour cream, salsa, etc.

Instructions

Given below are the detailed instructions for cooking this tasty meal on your air fryer. You need to follow these instructions in the given order.

- Heat oven to 425F.

- Start by preparing the potatoes. Put diced potatoes onto a baking sheet that has been lined with parchment paper or a silicone baking liner. Use your hands to mix the arrowroot powder, oil, paprika, onion powder, salt, and pepper, garlic powder into the potatoes until they are finely coated. Place the potatoes in the oven. Then bake for thirty minutes, stirring halfway through. When the potatoes are frying, prepare the rest of the fillings.

- To prepare the sausage, follow these steps: Over medium heat, heat a non-stick fry pan. As the ground pork cooks, choose a wooden spoon to break it up into small pieces. Cook, stirring regularly, for around six to seven minutes just until the meat is cooked through. Stir in the green chilies until well blended. Remove the prepared meat from the pan and place it on a plate.

- Reduce the heat to low-medium for the eggs. Whisk together the eggs, milk, salt, and pepper in a medium mixing bowl. Insert one tbsp butter and/or ghee into the same pan where the meat was fried. Add the eggs to the pan until the butter has melted. Continue moving the eggs with the help of a spatula over low heat till they thicken as well as a cook through. Turn off the heat and transfer the eggs to a cup.

- Assemble the burritos by assembling the tortillas, fried ground sausage, melted cheddar cheese and scrambled eggs. Fill with burrito with up to one and a half cup of filling. With each burrito, you may use about a half cup of beef, 1/3 cup of potatoes, 1/4 cup of scrambled eggs, and shredded cheese. Don't stuff the burritos too much.

- Wrap burritos: Roll tortillas and filling into a burrito that is tightly sealed and holds all of the fillings. Tighten the edges of the tortilla around each end of the filling. Push the bottom side of the tortilla up and on the filling with your thumbs, wrapping the sides you folded previously. Tuck the underside of the folded tortilla, as well as the sides from the top and bottom of the tortilla, into the burrito. Fold the left-over open tortilla over the folded sides and bottom of the burrito.

- To air fry, the burritos, carefully place two burritos in the basket of an air fryer. Preheat the oven to 350°F and air fry the burritos for six to ten minutes just until golden brown and crispy. Serve with salsa, whipped cream, chili sauce, and other toppings.

- The burritos can be stored in an airtight jar in the fridge for a maximum of four days. Air fry cold burritos at 325 degrees F for 14 to 18 minutes, or until crispy and golden brown along with a spritz of avocado spray oil.

2.6 Air-Fryer Bacon Crescent Rolls

Preparation time

20 minutes

Servings

8 persons

Nutritional facts

133 calories

Ingredients

We have listed below the ingredients that would be required by you for cooking this healthy and tasty meal on your home air fryer:

- One tube (8 ounces) refrigerated crescent rolls
- Six bacon strips, cooked and crumbled
- One teaspoon onion powder

Instructions

Given below are the detailed instructions for cooking this tasty meal on your air fryer. You need to follow these instructions in the given order.

- Heat air fryer to 300° F.
- Separate the crescent dough into 8 triangles after unrolling it. One tbsp of bacon should be put aside. Over the triangles, sprinkle the onion powder and the remaining bacon. Wrap it up and sprinkle the remaining bacon on top, gently pressing it in place.
  Place rolls point side down. These should be placed in a single layer on an ungreased tray in the air-fryer basket in batches. Cook for 8-10 minutes or until it is golden brown. Serve them warm.
- As far as freezing is concerned, you can put cooled rolls in freezer containers.
- Whenever you want to use them, first thaw at room temperature or microwave per roll on high for 10-15 seconds till heated through.

2.7 Air Fryer Donuts

Preparation time

2 hours 4 minutes

Servings

12 persons

Nutritional facts

251 calories

Ingredients

We have listed below the ingredients that would be required by you for cooking this healthy and tasty meal on your home air fryer:

- One cup milk, lukewarm (about 100°F)
- Two and a half teaspoons active dry yeast or instant yeast
- A quarter cup granulated sugar, plus 1 tsp
- A half tsp salt
- One egg
- A quarter cup unsalted butter, melted
- Three cups all-purpose flour
- Oil Spray, Coconut oil works best
- Six tbsp unsalted butter
- Two cups powdered sugar
- Two tsp vanilla extract
- Four tbsp hot water, or as needed

Instructions

Given below are the detailed instructions for cooking this tasty meal on your air fryer. You need to follow these instructions in the given order.

- Gently combine lukewarm milk, 1 teaspoon sugar, and yeast in the bowl of a stand mixer that is fitted with the dough handle. Allow 10 minutes for the foam to form (However, if nothing happens, then your milk was either too hot or the yeast was too old, you will have to start from the beginning).

- To the milk mixture, add the salt, sugar, egg, melted butter and 2 cups of flour. Mix on low speed until mixed, and then slowly add the remaining cup of flour as the mixer is working, till the dough no longer sticks to the bowl. Reduce the pace to low and knead the dough for 5 minutes or until it is elastic and soft.

- Cover the dough with plastic wrap after putting it in a greased bowl. Allow it to rise unless doubled in size in a warm location. If you make a dent in the dough with your finger and the indention remains, the dough is primed.

- Then move the dough out onto a floured board, punch it flat, and stretch it out to a thickness of around 1/2 inch. Then use a three-inch round cutter as well as a one-inch round cutter to slice the center, cut out 10-12 donuts.

- Place donuts and donut holes on parchment paper that has been gently floured and coated loosely with greased plastic wrap. Allow donuts to rise for 30 minutes or till they have doubled in size. Preheat the Air Fryer to three hundred- and fifty-degrees Fahrenheit.

- Spray the Air Fryer basket with oil spray and then gently move the donuts in a single layer to the basket. The donuts should be sprayed with oil spray and cooked at 350°F for 4 minutes or until golden brown. Rep with the rest of the donuts & holes.

- Melt butter in a shallow saucepan over medium heat when the donuts are in the Air Fryer. Combine powdered sugar as well as a vanilla extract in a mixing bowl and whisk until smooth. Remove from the fire and stir in one tablespoon of hot water at a time till the icing is thin but not watery. Then set aside.

- To submerge hot donuts & donut holes in glaze, use forks to dip them in. Let the excess glaze drip off on a wire rack spread over a rimmed baking dish. Allow ten minutes for the glaze to harden.

2.8 Air-Fryer French toast Cups with Raspberries

Preparation time

40 minutes

Servings

2 persons

Nutritional facts

406 calories

Ingredients

We have listed below the ingredients that would be required by you for cooking this healthy and tasty meal on your home air fryer:

- Two slices of Italian bread, cut into 1/2-inch cubes
- A half-cup fresh or frozen raspberries
- Two ounces cream cheese, cut into 1/2-inch cubes
- Two large eggs
- A half-cup whole milk
- One tablespoon maple syrup
- Two teaspoons cornstarch
- 1/3 cup water
- Two cups fresh or frozen raspberries, divided
- One tablespoon lemon juice
- One tablespoon maple syrup
- A half teaspoon grated lemon zest
- The ground cinnamon, optional

Instructions

Given below are the detailed instructions for cooking this tasty meal on your air fryer. You need to follow these instructions in the given order.

- Half of the bread cubes can be divided into two greased 8-ounce custard cups. Raspberries, as well as cream cheese, can be sprinkled on top. It can be topped with the remaining bread. Whisk together the eggs, milk, and syrup in a small bowl; sprinkle over the bread. Refrigerate for at least one hour after covering.

- Preheat the air fryer to three hundred- and twenty-five-degrees Fahrenheit. In an air-fryer basket, put custard cups. Cook for 12-15 minutes, or till golden brown & puffy.

- Meanwhile, whisk together cornstarch as well as water in a shallow saucepan till smooth. Combine 1-1/2 cup raspberries, sugar, lemon juice and lemon zest in a mixing bowl. Bring to a boil, and then turn off the heat. Cook and whisk for 2 minutes, or when the sauce has thickened. Strain out the seeds and set them aside to cool.

- Stir the remaining half cup of berries into the syrup gently. Sprinkle cinnamon on top of the French toast cups if needed, and then serve with maple syrup.

2.9 Air-Fryer Breakfast Croquettes with Egg & Asparagus

Preparation time

45 minutes

Servings

6 persons

Nutritional facts

294 calories

Ingredients

We have listed below the ingredients that would be required by you for cooking this healthy and tasty meal on your home air fryer:

- Three tablespoons butter
- Three tablespoons all-purpose flour
- Three-quarters cup 2% milk
- 6 large hard-boiled eggs, chopped
- A half-cup chopped fresh asparagus
- A half-cup chopped green onions
- A one-third cup shredded cheddar cheese
- 1 tablespoon minced fresh tarragon
- A quarter teaspoon of salt
- A quarter teaspoon of pepper
- One- and three-quarter cups panko bread crumbs
- Three large eggs, beaten
- Cooking spray

Instructions

Given below are the detailed instructions for cooking this tasty meal on your air fryer. You need to follow these instructions in the given order.

- Melt butter in a big saucepan over medium heat. Then cook as well as stir till finely browned, about 1-2 minutes after adding the flour. Gradually whisk in the milk and then simmer and stir until the sauce has thickened. Asparagus, cheese, green onions, hard-boiled eggs, tarragon, salt, and pepper are added to the blend. Refrigerate for a minimum of two hours before serving.

- Preheat the air fryer to three hundred- and fifty-degrees Fahrenheit. Make twelve three-inch-long ovals with 1/4 cup of the egg mixture. Separate the bread crumbs & eggs into small containers. To coat the logs, roll them in crumbs, then dip them in egg & roll them in crumbs again, patting to make the coating adhere.

- Put croquettes in the form of a single layer on a greased tray in the air-fryer basket in batches; spritz with cooking spray. Cook for 8-10 minutes until it's golden brown. Spritz with the cooking spray. Cook for another 3-5 minutes till it's golden brown.

2.10 Air Fryer Breakfast Frittata

Preparation time

35 minutes

Servings

2 persons

Nutritional facts

380 calories

Ingredients

We have listed below the ingredients that would be required by you for cooking this healthy and tasty food in the air fryer:

- Quarter pound breakfast sausage fully cooked and crumbled
- One pinch of cayenne pepper (Optional)
- cooking spray
- Four eggs, lightly beaten
- half cup shredded Cheddar-Monterey Jack cheese blend
- Two tablespoons red bell pepper, diced
- One green onion, chopped

Instructions

Given below are the detailed instructions for cooking this tasty food in the air fryer. You need to follow these instructions in the given order.

- Mix well in small bowl eggs, sausage, cheddar cheese, cayenne, bell pepper and onion.
- Heat the air fryer to 360 °F (180 degrees C).
- Next, a nonstick cake pan is to be sprayed with cooking spray.
- Put the egg mixture in the cake pan.
- Then cook it in the air for eighteen to twenty minutes fryer till frittata is set.

2.11 Ninja Foodi Low-Carb Breakfast Casserole Air Fryer

Preparation time

45 minutes

Servings

8 persons

Nutritional facts

182 calories

Ingredients

We have listed below the ingredients that would be required by you for cooking this healthy and tasty food in the air fryer:

- One teaspoon Fennel Seed
- One-pound Ground Sausage
- A quarter cup Diced White Onion
- A half-cup Shredded Colby Jack Cheese
- 1 Diced Green Bell Pepper
- 8 Whole Eggs, Beaten
- A half teaspoon Garlic Salt

Instructions

Given below are the detailed instructions for cooking this tasty food in the air fryer. You need to follow these instructions in the given order.

- Use the saute feature to brown the sausage in the food pot if you are using the Ninja Foodi. You can use a skillet to do this if you are using an air-fryer.
- Insert the onion and pepper and simmer until the vegetables are soft and the sausage is cooked, along with the ground sausage.
- Spray an 8.75 inches pan and/or the air fryer with the cooking spray.
- Place the mixture of ground sausages on the bottom of the pan.
- Cover with cheese uniformly.
- Pour the beaten eggs uniformly over the sausage and cheese.

- Over the eggs, add fennel seed and garlic salt uniformly.
- In Ninja Foodi, put the rack in the low position and then place the pan on top.
- Set at 390 degrees F for 15 minutes on Air Crisp.
- If you are using an air fryer, put the dish straight into the air fryer's basket and cook at 390 degrees F for 15 minutes.
- Remove and serve wisely.

2.12 Air Fryer Donuts

Preparation time

15 minutes

Servings

8 persons

Nutritional facts

316 calories

Ingredients

We have listed below the ingredients that would be required by you for cooking this healthy and tasty food in the air fryer:

- Half cup granulated white sugar
- Two teaspoons ground cinnamon
- 4 Tablespoons butter melted
- 16 oz refrigerated flaky jumbo biscuits
- olive or coconut oil spray

Instructions

Given below are the detailed instructions for cooking this tasty food in the air fryer. You need to follow these instructions in the given order.

- Combine in a small bowl sugar and cinnamon; set aside.
- The biscuits are withdrawn from the can, divided and placed on a flat surface. To cut holes out of the middle of each biscuit, use a 1-inch round biscuit cutter (or similar-sized bottle cap).
- Cover the air fryer basket lightly with olive or coconut oil spray. Do not use a non-stick spray like Pam, as the coating on the basket may be damaged.
- Put four donuts in a single layer in the basket of the air fryer. Ensure that they are not touching.
- Then air fry for five minutes at 360 degrees and/ or till lightly browned.
- The donuts are to be removed from Air Fryer. Then dip them in melted butter. Next, roll them in cinnamon sugar to coat. Serve immediately.

2.13 Wrapped Vegan Bacon Mini Breakfast Burritos

Preparation time

55 minutes

Servings

4 persons

Nutritional facts

184 calories

Ingredients

We have listed below the ingredients that would be required by you for cooking this healthy and tasty food in the air fryer:

- Two tbsp. cashew butter
- Two to three tbsp. tamari
- One to Two tbsp. liquid smoke
- 1 small sautéed tree broccoli,
- 6 to 8 stalks of fresh asparagus
- Handful kale, spinach and other greens
- One to Two tablespoons water
- 4 pieces of rice paper
- Two servings **Vegan Egg** scramble or **Tofu Scramble**
- One-third cup sweet potato cubes, roasted
- 8 strips red pepper, roasted

Instructions

Given below are the detailed instructions for cooking this tasty food in the air fryer. You need to follow these instructions in the given order.

- Preheat the oven to 350 degrees F. Line with the parchment of the baking dish.
- Whisk together the cashew butter, liquid smoke, tamari, and water in a small bowl. Then put aside.
- Prepare to make rolls for all fillings.

- Rice Paper Hydrating: have a big plate ready for filling/rolling wrapper. Keep 1 rice paper under a water faucet that runs cool water, wetting both sides of the wrapper for few seconds. Then it should be removed from the water. While it is still firm, it should be placed on a plate to fill. Subsequently, the rice paper will soften as it sits. However, it will not be too tender to stick to the surface.

- Then it is to be filled by putting ingredients away from the middle. Ensure to leave sides of rice paper open. Fold in two sides just like a burrito. Each roll is to be dipped into a cashew liquid smoke mix. You have to ensure to coat it completely. Then the rolls are to be arranged on a parchment baking sheet.

- Now cook these for eight to ten minutes at 350 °F and till it becomes crisp.

2.14 Air Fryer Breakfast Sausage

Preparation time

20 minutes

Servings

8 persons

Nutritional facts

188 calories

Ingredients

We have listed below the ingredients that would be required by you for cooking this healthy and tasty food in the air fryer:

- One pound ground pork
- One pound ground turkey
- Two teaspoons fennel seeds
- Two teaspoons dry rubbed sage
- Two teaspoons garlic powder
- One teaspoon paprika
- One teaspoon sea salt
- One teaspoon dried thyme
- One tablespoon real maple syrup

Instructions

Given below are the detailed instructions for cooking this tasty food in the air fryer. You need to follow these instructions in the given order.

- Start by combining in a wide bowl the pork and turkey together. Mix the rest of the ingredients together in a small bowl: fennel, sage, salt, powdered garlic, paprika and thyme. Mix spices into the meat and keep combining until the spices are thoroughly blended.

- Spoon (about 2-3 teaspoons of meat) into balls, then flatten into patties. You would actually have to do this in two batches.

- Fix the temperature and cook for 10 minutes at 370 degrees F. Remove and repeat for the leftover sausage in the air fryer.

2.15 Wake Up Air Fryer Avocado Boats

Preparation time

5 minutes

Servings

2 persons

Nutritional facts

122 calories

Ingredients

We have listed below the ingredients that would be required by you for cooking this healthy and tasty food in the air fryer:

- A quarter cup red onion, diced
- Two tbsp. fresh cilantro chopped
- 2 plum tomatoes, seeded and diced
- 4 eggs (medium or large recommended)
- 1 tbsp. jalapeno, finely diced (optional)
- 1 tbsp. lime juice
- 1/2 tsp. salt
- A quarter tsp black pepper
- 2 avocados, halved and pitted

Instructions

Given below are the detailed instructions for cooking this tasty food in the air fryer. You need to follow these instructions in the given order.

- Spoon the avocado pulp out of the skin, keeping the shell unbroken. Dice the avocado and put it in a bowl. Combine the tomatoes, cilantro, onion, jalapeno, lime juice, salt, and pepper, if needed. Cover and refrigerate the mixture of avocado until ready for use.
- The air fryer is preheated to 350 °F.
- Place them on a foil ring to be sure that avocado shells do not rock while

cooking. Just roll two 3-inch-wide strips of aluminum foil into rope shape to make them, and form each into a 3-inch circle. In an air fryer basket, place each avocado shell on a foil ring. Break one egg into each shell of avocado and fry for 5 - 7 minutes or until the doneness is achieved.

- Remove from the basket; top with salsa the avocado and serve.

2.16 Crispy Bacon in the Air Fryer

Preparation time

10 minutes

Servings

12 persons

Nutritional facts

177 calories

Ingredients

We have listed below the ingredients that would be required by you for cooking this healthy and tasty food in the air fryer:

- One Pound of Bacon

Instructions

Given below are the detailed instructions for cooking this tasty food in the air fryer. You need to follow these instructions in the given order.

- Add bacon uniformly into the air fryer basket. This can require two batches to cook all the bacon, depending on size.
- Cook for 5 minutes at 350 degrees F.
- Flip the bacon and cook for an additional five minutes or until the crispiness you prefer.
- Remove the bacon with tongs and put it on a plate lined with paper towels.
- Allow it to cool and serve.

2.17 Ninja Foodi - Air Fryer Breakfast Stuffed Peppers

Preparation time

18 minutes

Servings

2 persons

Nutritional facts

164 calories

Ingredients

We have listed below the ingredients that would be required by you for cooking this healthy and tasty food in the air fryer:

- 4 **eggs**
- One teaspoon **olive oil**
- One bell pepper cut; middle seeds detached
- One pinch of **salt and pepper**
- One pinch sriracha flakes for spice, optional

Instructions

Given below are the detailed instructions for cooking this tasty food in the air fryer. You need to follow these instructions in the given order.

- Bell peppers should be cut in half lengthwise and the seeds and center removed, but the sides should be left intact like plates.
- Apply a small amount of olive oil to the raw edges with your hand (where it was cut).
- In each bell pepper half, break two eggs. Season with the spices of your preference.
- Place them on a trivet or directly inside your Ninja Foodi or other types of the air fryer.
- Close the cover on your air fryer (the one you're using right now).
- Switch on the machine and set the air crisper to 390 degrees for 13 minutes (times will differ slightly accordingly).

- Alternatively, if you want your bell pepper and egg to be less brown on the outside, add only one egg to your pepper and cook for 15 minutes at 330°F in an air fryer. (for a hard-boiled egg consistency)

2.18 Quick Air Fryer Breakfast Pockets - Hand Held Hot Breakfast Recipe

Preparation time

20 minutes

Servings

8 persons

Nutritional facts

170 calories

Ingredients

We have listed below the ingredients that would be required by you for cooking this healthy and tasty food in the air fryer:

- 5 eggs
- A half-cup sausage crumbles, cooked
- Half cup bacon, cooked
- one box puff pastry sheets
- A half-cup cheddar cheese, shredded

Instructions

Given below are the detailed instructions for cooking this tasty food in the air fryer. You need to follow these instructions in the given order.

- Cook eggs in the form of regular scrambled eggs. If desired, add meat to the egg mixture while you are cooking.
- Spread puff pastry sheets on a cutting board and use a cookie cutter or knife to cut out rectangles, making sure they are all uniform, so they fit together nicely.
- Spoon half of the pastry rectangles with the preferred combination of egg, meat, and cheese.
- Place a rectangle of pastry on top of the mixture and press the edges together with a sealing fork.
- Spray with spray oil if a shiny, smooth pastry is desired, but it is really optional.

- Place breakfast pockets in the air-fryer basket and cook at 370 degrees for 8-10 minutes.
- Carefully watch and check for desired doneness every 2-3 minutes.

2.19 Air Fryer Bacon and Egg Breakfast Biscuit Bombs

Preparation time

50 minutes

Servings

8 persons

Nutritional facts

200 calories

Ingredients

We have listed below the ingredients that would be required by you for cooking this healthy and tasty food in the air fryer:

- 2 beaten eggs
- A quarter tsp pepper
- 5 biscuits
- 2 oz cheddar cheese, cut into ten 3/4-inch cubes
- One egg
- 4 slices bacon, cut into 1/2-inch pieces
- 1 tablespoon butter
- One tablespoon water

Instructions

Given below are the detailed instructions for cooking this tasty food in the air fryer. You need to follow these instructions in the given order.

- Slice two 8-inch rounds of parchment paper for cooking. Set one round at the bottom of the basket of the air fryer. Spray with cooking spray.
- In a nonstick 10-inch skillet, cook bacon until crisp over medium-high heat.
- Place on a paper towel; remove from the pan. Wipe the skillet carefully with a paper towel. To the skillet, add butter and melt over medium heat. Add 2 beaten eggs and pepper to the skillet; cook until the eggs are condensed, stirring frequently, but still moist. Remove from the heat; add bacon and stir. Cool for five minutes.

49

- Meanwhile, divide the dough into five biscuits; separate the 2 layers of each biscuit. Press into a 4-inch round each. Then spoon 1 onto the center of each round heaping tablespoonful of the egg mixture. Top it with one of the cheese pieces. Fold the edges gently up and over the filling, squeeze to seal. Beat the remainder of the egg and water in a small bowl. Brush the biscuits with egg wash on all sides.

- Place 5 biscuit bombs on the parchment in the air fryer basket, seam side down. With cooking spray, spray both sides of the second round of parchment. Top the biscuit bombs in the basket with 2nd parchment, then top with the leftover 5 biscuit bombs.

- Set to 325-degree F; cook for eight minutes. Removes the top of the round parchment; use tongs to carefully turn the biscuits and place them in a single layer in the basket. Cook 4 - 6 more minutes or (at least 165°F) until cooked through.

CHAPTER 3: Air Fryer Lunch Recipes

This chapter contains a collection of tasty lunch recipes that you can easily make in the air fryer.

3.1 Air-Fryer Southern-Style Chicken

Preparation time

35 minutes

Servings

6 persons

Nutritional facts

410 calories

Ingredients

We have listed below the ingredients that would be required by you for cooking this healthy and tasty meal on your home air fryer:

- Two cups crushed Ritz crackers (about 50)
- One tablespoon minced fresh parsley
- One teaspoon garlic salt
- One teaspoon paprika
- 1/2 teaspoon pepper
- A one-fourth teaspoon of ground cumin
- A one-fourth teaspoon rubbed sage
- One large egg, beaten
- One broiler/fryer chicken (3 to 4 pounds), cut up
- Cooking spray

Instructions

Given below are the detailed instructions for cooking this tasty meal on your air fryer. You need to follow these instructions in the given order.

- Heat air fryer to 375° F.

- Blend the first seven ingredients in a bowl dish. In another shallow bowl, place the egg. Dip the chicken in the egg and then in the cracker paste, patting it down to make the coating firm on them. Put chicken in the form of a single layer on a greased tray in the air-fryer basket in batches, spritzed with cooking spray.

- Cook for ten minutes. Cook, turning chicken once more and spritzing with cooking mist, until golden brown, so juices run free, ten to twenty minutes longer.

3.2 Garlic-Rosemary Brussels Sprouts

Preparation time

30 minutes

Servings

4 persons

Nutritional facts

164 calories

Ingredients

We have listed below the ingredients that would be required by you for cooking this healthy and tasty meal on your home air fryer:

- Three tbsp. olive oil

- 2 minced garlic cloves,

- A one-half teaspoon salts

- A one-fourth teaspoon of pepper

- 1 pound Brussels sprouts, cut and trimmed

- A half-cup panko breadcrumbs

- One and a half teaspoon fresh rosemary, minced

Instructions

Given below are the detailed instructions for cooking this tasty meal on your air fryer. You need to follow these instructions in the given order.

- Heat air fryer to 350° F.

- In a shallow microwave-safe bowl, combine the first four ingredients: microwave for 30 seconds.

- In two teaspoons oil mixture, toss Brussels sprouts. Cook 4-5 minutes with Brussels sprouts on a tray in an air-fryer basket. Sprouts can be stirred. Cook, mixing halfway through cooking time until sprouts are gently golden and near-ideal tenderness, around 8 minutes.

- Combine bread crumbs, rosemary, and the remaining oil mixture.

- Then sprinkle on sprouts. Cook for another 3-5 minutes, or until the crumbs have browned and the sprouts are cooked. Serve straight away.

3.3 Air-Fryer Fish and Fries

Preparation time

25 minutes

Servings

4 persons

Nutritional facts

312 calories

Ingredients

We have listed below the ingredients that would be required by you for cooking this healthy and tasty meal on your home air fryer:

- One-pound potatoes (about 2 medium)
- 2 tablespoons olive oil
- A one-fourth teaspoon of pepper
- A one-fourth teaspoon of salt
- 1/3 cup all-purpose flour
- A one-fourth teaspoon of pepper
- One large egg
- 2 tablespoons water
- A two-third cup crushed cornflakes
- One tablespoon grated Parmesan cheese
- 1/8 teaspoon cayenne pepper
- A one-fourth teaspoon of salt
- One pound haddock or cod fillets
- Tartar sauce, optional

Instructions

Given below are the detailed instructions for cooking this tasty meal on your air fryer. You need to follow these instructions in the given order.

- Heat air fryer to 400° F.

- Potatoes should be peeled and sliced lengthwise into 1/2-inch-thick strips and cut into 1/2-inch-thick sticks.

- Mix potatoes with oil, pepper, and salt in a large mixing bowl. Put potatoes in the form of a single layer on a tray in an air-fryer basket in batches and cook until only tender, around 5-10 minutes. Toss potatoes and roast for another 5-10 minutes, or until finely browned and crisp.

- Meanwhile, combine flour as well as pepper in a shallow bowl. Whisk the egg with the water in a small dish. Toss cornflakes along with cheese & cayenne in a third bowl. Season the fish with salt and pepper, then dunk it in the flour mixture to cover both sides and shake off the excess. Dip in the egg mixture, then in the cornflake mixture, patting to ensure that the coating sticks.

- Remove the fries from the basket and keep them warm. Place the fish on a tray in the air-fryer basket on a single sheet. Cook for eight to ten minutes, turning halfway through until the fish is gently browned and flaking easily with a fork. Don't overcook the food. Transfer the fries to the basket to finish frying. Serve right away. It can be served with tartar sauce if desired.

3.4 Air-Fryer Pickles

Preparation time

35 minutes

Servings

22 pickle slices

Nutritional facts

26 calories per pickle slice

Ingredients

We have listed below the ingredients that would be required by you for cooking this healthy and tasty meal on your home air fryer:

- 32 dill pickle slices
- A half teaspoon garlic powder
- 2 cups panko bread crumbs
- 2 tablespoons snipped fresh dill
- Cooking spray
- A half-cup all-purpose flour
- A half teaspoon of salt
- 3 large eggs, lightly beaten
- 2 tablespoons dill pickle juice
- A half teaspoon of cayenne pepper
- Ranch salad dressing, optional

Instructions

Given below are the detailed instructions for cooking this tasty meal on your air fryer. You need to follow these instructions in the given order.

- Preheat air fryer to 400° F.
- Leave pickles to remain on a paper towel for about 15 minutes or until the liquid has almost entirely disappeared.
- Meanwhile, mix flour & salt in a shallow bowl. Stir pickle juice, eggs, cayenne

pepper, and garlic powder together in a shallow bowl. In a third shallow bowl, combine panko and dill.

- Shake off extra flour after dipping pickles in flour mixture on both ends. Dip in the egg mixture, then in the crumb mixture, patting to ensure that the coating sticks. Put pickles in the form of a single layer on a greased tray in the air-fryer basket in batches. Cook for 7-10 minutes, or till golden brown and crispy. Turn the pickles over and spritz them with cooking oil. Cook for another 7-10 minutes, or till golden brown and crispy. Serve right away. Serve with ranch dressing if needed.

3.5 Air-Fryer Mini Nutella Doughnut Holes

Preparation time

35 minutes

Servings

32 doughnuts

Nutritional facts

94 calories

Ingredients

We have listed below the ingredients that would be required by you for cooking this healthy and tasty meal on your home air fryer:

- One large egg
- One tablespoon water
- One tube (16.3 ounces) large cold, flaky biscuits (8 counts)
- A two-third cup Nutella
- Oil
- Confectioners' sugar

Instructions

Given below are the detailed instructions for cooking this tasty meal on your air fryer. You need to follow these instructions in the given order.

- Heat air fryer to 300° F.
- Combine the egg and water in a mixing bowl. Roll each biscuit into a 6-inch circle on a finely floured surface and cut into four wedges. Brush each wedge gently with the egg mixture and one tsp Nutella. Bring up the corners over the filling and tightly pinch the edges to seal.
- Assemble biscuits on a single sheet on an ungreased tray in the air-fryer basket in batches. Cook for 8-10 minutes, rotating once, till golden brown. Serve wet, dusted with confectioners' sugar.

3.6 Air-Fryer Ground Beef Wellington

Preparation time

50 minutes

Servings

2 persons

Nutritional facts

585 calories

Ingredients

We have listed below the ingredients that would be required by you for cooking this healthy and tasty meal on your home air fryer:

- One tablespoon butter
- A half-cup chopped fresh mushrooms
- two teaspoons all-purpose flour
- A one fourth teaspoon pepper, divided
- A half-cup half-and-half cream
- One large egg yolk
- Two tablespoons finely chopped onion
- A one-fourth teaspoon of salt
- A half-pound ground beef
- One tube (4 ounces) refrigerated crescent rolls
- 1 large egg, lightly beaten, optional
- One teaspoon dried parsley flakes

Instructions

Given below are the detailed instructions for cooking this tasty meal on your air fryer. You need to follow these instructions in the given order.

- Heat air fryer to 300° F.
- Melt butter in a saucepan on medium-high heat. Cook, as well as stir till the mushrooms are soft, around five to six minutes. Blend in the flour and one-

eighth teaspoon pepper till just combined. Gradually pour in the milk. Bring to a boil, then reduce to low heat and simmer, constantly stirring, for 2 minutes, or until the sauce has thickened. Take the pan off the heat and set it aside.

- Combine the egg yolk, carrot, 2 teaspoons mushroom sauce, salt, and the remaining one-eighth tsp pepper in a mixing bowl. Mix in the beef crumbles thoroughly. Divide the dough into two loaves. Unroll the crescent dough and cut it into two rectangles, sealing the perforations. Place a meat loaf in the center of every rectangle. Pinch the sides together to secure them. Rub with beaten egg if necessary.

- Place Wellingtons in an air-fryer basket in a single layer on a greased tray. Cook for 18-22 minutes, until its golden brown as well as a thermometer inserted into the meat loaf, reads 160° F.

- In the meantime, warm the remaining sauce at low heat and add the parsley. With the Wellingtons, serve the sauce.

3.7 Air Fryer-Egg in Hole

Preparation time

15 minutes

Servings

1 person

Nutritional facts

130 calories

Ingredients

We have listed below the ingredients that would be required by you for cooking this healthy and tasty food in the air fryer:

- One piece of toast
- One egg
- salt and pepper

Instructions

Given below are the detailed instructions for cooking this tasty food in the air fryer. You need to follow these instructions in the given order.

- Oil the air fryer-safe pan with cooking spray that is non-stick.
- Place your slice of bread in the air fryer pan.
- Create a hole with a cup. Then the bread is to be removed.
- Crack the egg in the hole.
- Then air fry for 6 minutes at 330 degrees F. Then take a spatula to flip the egg and fry for another three to four minutes.

3.8 Air fryer French toast Sticks Recipe

Preparation time

17 minutes

Servings

2 persons

Nutritional facts

178 calories

Ingredients

We have listed below the ingredients that would be required by you for cooking this healthy and tasty food in the air fryer:

- 4 pieces bread (whatever kind and thickness desired)
- 1 pinch nutmeg
- 1 pinch ground cloves
- 2 Tablespoons butter (or margarine, softened)
- 2 eggs (gently beaten)
- 1 pinch salt
- 1 pinch **cinnamon**
- One teaspoon icing sugar (and/or maple syrup for garnish and serving)

Instructions

Given below are the detailed instructions for cooking this tasty food in the air fryer. You need to follow these instructions in the given order.

- Heat Air fryer to 180 degrees Celsius.
- In a bowl, softly beat together with a sprinkle of salt, two eggs, a few hard shakes of cinnamon, and tiny pinches of both nutmeg and ground cloves.
- Butter the bread slices on both sides and cut them into strips.
- Dredge and arrange each strip in the Air Fryer in the egg mixture (you will have to cook in two batches).
- Stop the Air Fryer after 2 minutes of frying, remove the plate, ensure that you

put the pan on a heat-safe surface. Then spray the bread with cooking spray.

- Once you get the strips generously sprayed, also flip and spray the second side.

- Return the pan to the fryer and cook for another 4 minutes, testing after a few minutes to ensure that it cooks evenly and does not burn.

- Remove from the Air Fryer and serve if the egg is fried and the bread is golden brown.

- Sprinkle with icing sugar for garnishing and serving, top with cream or drizzle with maple syrup.

3.9 Bacon Wrapped Avocado

Preparation time

5 minutes

Servings

24 persons

Nutritional facts

120 calories

Ingredients

We have listed below the ingredients that would be required by you for cooking this healthy and tasty food in the air fryer:

- Three avocados

- Twenty-four thin strips of bacon

- A quarter cup ranch dressing for serving

Instructions

Given below are the detailed instructions for cooking this tasty food in the air fryer. You need to follow these instructions in the given order.

- Slice every avocado into eight wedges of equal size. Wrap each wedge with a bacon strip and, if necessary, cut the bacon.

- Working in batches, place in a single layer in an air fryer basket. Cook for 8 minutes at 400 °F until the bacon is fried and crispy.

- Serve warm along with the ranch.

3.10 Antipasto Egg Rolls

Preparation time

30 minutes

Servings

12 persons

Nutritional facts

280 calories

Ingredients

We have listed below the ingredients that would be required by you for cooking this healthy and tasty food in the air fryer:

- Twelve egg roll wrappers
- Twelve slices provolone
- 1 cup shredded mozzarella
- 1 cup sliced Pepperoncini
- Twelve slices of deli ham
- 36 slices pepperoni
- 1/4 cup freshly grated Parmesan
- Italian dressing, for serving

Instructions

Given below are the detailed instructions for cooking this tasty food in the air fryer. You need to follow these instructions in the given order.

- Put an egg roll wrapper in a diamond shape place on a clean. Then it is to be topped with one 3 slices of pepperoni, a slice of ham and a large pinch of both pepperoncini and mozzarella. Now the bottom half is to be folded up. Then tightly fold in sides. Roll gently. Then seal the fold with a few drops of water.
- Working in batches, Cook egg rolls for 12 minutes at 390° F or until golden. Do not forget to flip halfway.

3.11 Cauliflower Tots

Preparation time

30 minutes

Servings

6 persons

Nutritional facts

340 calories

Ingredients

We have listed below the ingredients that would be required by you for cooking this healthy and tasty food in the air fryer:

- 1 cup shredded cheddar
- Half cup ketchup
- 2 tablespoons. Sriracha
- 1 cup freshly grated Parmesan
- 2/3 cup panko breadcrumbs
- 2 tablespoons. freshly chopped chives
- Cooking spray
- Four cup steamed cauliflower florets (about 1/2 cauliflower)
- 1 large egg, lightly beaten
- Kosher salt
- Freshly ground black pepper

Instructions

Given below are the detailed instructions for cooking this tasty food in the air fryer. You need to follow these instructions in the given order.

- Process steamed cauliflower in a food processor till riced. Put riced cauliflower on a clean kitchen towel. Then squeeze to drain water.
- Move cauliflower to a big bowl with panko, egg, cheddar, Parmesan and chives. Now mix till combined. Season with pepper and salt as per the requirement.

- One tablespoon mixture is to be spooned and rolled into a tater-tot shape using your hands. Working in batches. Now, these have to be arranged in a single layer in the air fryer basket.

- Then cook for ten minutes at 375° F or until tots turn golden.

- Prepare spicy ketchup by combining ketchup and Sriracha in a small serving bowl. Stir well to mix.

- Enjoy warm cauliflower tots along with spicy ketchup.

3.12 Cheesy Beef Empanadas

Preparation time

2 hours

Servings

15 persons

Nutritional facts

456 calories

Ingredients

We have listed below the ingredients that would be required by you for cooking this healthy and tasty food in the air fryer:

- Half cup cold butter, cut into cubes
- 3/4 cup water
- 1 large egg
- 1 tablespoon extra-virgin olive oil
- 1 yellow onion, chopped
- 2 cloves garlic, minced
- 3 cup all-purpose flour, plus more for surface
- 1 tsp kosher salt
- 1 tsp baking powder
- 1 lb. ground beef
- 1 tablespoon tomato paste
- 1 tsp oregano
- 1 tsp cumin
- Egg wash for brushing
- Freshly chopped cilantro for garnish
- Sour cream, for serving
- A half teaspoon. paprika
- Kosher salt

- Freshly ground black pepper
- Half cup chopped tomatoes
- Half cup chopped pickled jalapeños
- 1 1/4 cup shredded Cheddar
- 1 1/4 cup Shredded Monterey Jack

Instructions

Given below are the detailed instructions for cooking this tasty food in the air fryer. You need to follow these instructions in the given order.

- Whisk the salt, flour, and baking powder together in a big bowl. Use your hands or a pastry cutter to cut the butter into the flour until. Add the egg and water and combine until it forms a dough. Turn the dough on a lightly floured surface and knead for around 5 minutes until soft.

- Wrap up and refrigerate for at least one hour in plastic wrap.

- Heat oil in a large skillet over medium heat. Add the onion & cook until soft, about 5 minutes, then add the garlic and cook for 1 more minute, until fragrant. Add the ground beef and cook for 5 minutes, breaking the meat with a wooden spoon until it is no longer pink. Fat is to be drained.

- Return the pan to medium heat and stir in the beef with the tomato paste. Season with salt and pepper and add oregano, cumin, and paprika. Add the tomatoes and jalapeños and cook for about 3 minutes, until hot. Remove from heat and allow it to cool slightly.
  On a lightly floured surface, put the dough and divide it in half. Cut out rounds using a 4½ round cookie cutter." Repeat with the dough that remains.

- Lightly moisten the outer edge of a dough round with water and put around two tablespoons of cheddar and Monterey filling in the middle and top. Fold dough in half over the filling. Fold the edges together with a fork. Then brush them with egg wash. Repeat with the leftover dough and filling.

- Put empanadas in a parchment-lined Air Fryer basket to ensure they do not touch, and cook for 10 minutes in batches at 400 ° F.

- It is to be garnished with cilantro. Finally, serve with sour cream.

3.13 Homemade Cannoli

Preparation time

3 hours

Servings

20 persons

Nutritional facts

160 calories

Ingredients

We have listed below the ingredients that would be required by you for cooking this healthy and tasty food in the air fryer:

- Half cup powdered sugar, divided
- 3/4 cup heavy cream
- 6 tablespoons. white wine
- 1 large egg
- 1 egg white for brushing
- Vegetable oil for frying
- 1 tsp pure vanilla extract
- 1 tsp orange zest
- 1/4 tsp kosher salt
- Half cup mini chocolate chips, for garnish
- Two cups flour, plus more for surface
- 1 (16-oz.) container ricotta
- Half cup mascarpone cheese
- 1/4 cup granulated sugar
- 1 tsp kosher salt
- A half teaspoon. cinnamon
- 4 tbsp. cold butter, cut into cubes

Instructions

Given below are the detailed instructions for cooking this tasty food in the air fryer. You need to follow these instructions in the given order.

- By placing a fine-mesh strainer over a wide bowl, drain the ricotta. Let it drain for at least an hour in the refrigerator and up to overnight.

- Using a hand mixer, mix heavy cream and a quarter cup of powdered sugar in a large bowl until stiff peaks appear.

- Combine ricotta, mascarpone, a quarter of a cup of powdered sugar, salt, vanilla and orange zest in another large bowl. Fold the whipped cream into it. Refrigerate for at least 1 hour until ready to fill with cannoli.

- Whisk the flour, sugar, salt, and cinnamon together in a big bowl. Using your hands or pastry cutter, cut butter into the flour mixture until pea-sized. Add the wine and egg and combine until it forms a dough. To make the dough come together, knead a few times in the bowl. Pat into a flat circle, cover and refrigerate for at least 1 hour and up to overnight in plastic wrap.

- Divide the dough into halves on a lightly floured surface. Roll to 1/8" thick. To cut out dough, use a 4-circle cookie cutter. Repeat with the dough that remains. To cut a few extra circles, re-roll the scraps.

- Wrap cannoli molds and brush egg whites around the dough where the dough will join to seal together.

- Working in batches, put molds in air fryer baskets and cook for 12 minutes or until golden at 350 ° F.

- Remove twist shells gently from molds when cool enough to handle or use a kitchen towel to hold them.

- The pipe is filled into shells and then dipped into mini chocolate chips.

- Put filling in a pastry bag. It should be fitted with an open star tip. The filling is to be piped into shells. Next, dip ends in mini chocolate chips and enjoy.

3.14 Twice Baked Potatoes

Preparation time

2 hours

Servings

6 persons

Nutritional facts

179 calories

Ingredients

We have listed below the ingredients that would be required by you for cooking this healthy and tasty food in the air fryer:

- Kosher salt
- Half cup (1 stick) butter, softened
- Half cup milk
- Half cup sour cream
- 1 Half cup shredded Cheddar, divided
- 2 green onions, thinly sliced, plus more for garnish
- 6 large russet potatoes, scrubbed clean
- 1 tablespoon extra-virgin olive oil
- Freshly ground black pepper

Instructions

Given below are the detailed instructions for cooking this tasty food in the air fryer. You need to follow these instructions in the given order.

- Pat potatoes with paper towels fully dry. With a fork, poke the potatoes all over, then brush them with oil & sprinkle with salt. Acting in batches, put the potatoes in an air fryer basket and cook for 40 minutes at 400 ° F. Place it on a big baking sheet and allow it to cool until cool enough to treat.
- Cutting lengthwise, cut off the top of each potato a thin layer. Scoop out of each potato, leaving a 1/2" border. Place the insides of it in a big bowl. Keep the tops of the potatoes and roast them as a snack on the tray!

- Add sour cream, butter and milk and smash until butter is melted and potatoes are almost smooth, but with some chunks, to bowl with potatoes. Insert 1 cup of the green onions and cheese and stir until combined. With salt and pepper, season.

- Cover the baked potatoes with potato mixture as well as put them back in the air fryer basket. Top with half a cup of cheddar left. Cook for 5 minutes at 400 °F until the cheese is melted and crispy outside.

- Garnish prior to serving with more green onions.

3.15 Air Fryer Steak

Preparation time

45 minutes

Servings

2 persons

Nutritional facts

460 calories

Ingredients

We have listed below the ingredients that would be required by you for cooking this healthy and tasty food in the air fryer:

- Two teaspoons freshly chopped parsley
- Kosher salt
- Freshly ground black pepper
- 1 tsp freshly chopped chives
- 1 tsp freshly chopped thyme
- 1 tsp freshly chopped rosemary
- 4 tablespoons butter, softened
- 2 cloves garlic, minced
- 1 (2 lb.) bone-in ribeye

Instructions

Given below are the detailed instructions for cooking this tasty food in the air fryer. You need to follow these instructions in the given order.

- Combine the butter and spices in a shallow bowl. Place it in the middle of the plastic piece middle and roll it into a log. The twist ends together. It should be refrigerated for twenty minutes till hardened.

- Season the steak with salt and pepper on both sides.

- Put the steak in the air fryer basket and cook at 400 ° F for twelve to fourteen minutes, for medium, based on steak thickness, flipping halfway through.

- Top steak with a herb butter slice.

3.16 Air Fryer Brownies

Preparation time

35 minutes

Servings

2 persons

Nutritional facts

195 calories

Ingredients

We have listed below the ingredients that would be required by you for cooking this healthy and tasty food in the air fryer:

- Half cup granulated sugar
- One third cup cocoa powder
- 1/4 cup butter, melted and cooled slightly
- 1 large egg
- 1/4 cup all-purpose flour
- 1/4 tsp baking powder
- Pinch kosher salt

Instructions

Given below are the detailed instructions for cooking this tasty food in the air fryer. You need to follow these instructions in the given order.

- Grease a 6-inch diameter cake pan with cooking spray. Whisk in a medium bowl to mix sugar, salt, chocolate powder, flour and baking powder.

- Whisk the melted butter and egg in a small bowl until mixed. To dry ingredients, add wet ingredients and stir till combined.

- Move brownie batter to the prepared cake pan as well as the smooth top. Cook for 16-18 minutes in the air fryer at 350 ° F. Before slicing, let cool for 10 minutes.

3.17 Spicy Chicken Taquitos

Preparation time

45 minutes

Servings

12 persons

Nutritional facts

160 calories

Ingredients

We have listed below the ingredients that would be required by you for cooking this healthy and tasty food in the air fryer:

- 1 tsp. cumin
- 1 tsp. chili powder
- Kosher salt
- Cooking spray
- 3 cups shredded cooked chicken
- 1 (8-oz.) block cream cheese, softened
- Freshly ground black pepper
- 1 chipotle in adobo sauce, chopped, plus 1 tablespoon sauce
- 12 small corn tortillas
- One and a Half cup shredded cheddar
- One and a Half cup shredded Pepper Jack
- Pico de Gallo, for serving
- 1 clove garlic
- Juice of lime
- Kosher salt
- Freshly ground black pepper
- Crumbled queso fresco for serving
- For the avocado cream sauce

- 1 large avocado, pitted
- Half cup sour cream
- 1/4 cup packed cilantro leaves

Instructions

Given below are the detailed instructions for cooking this tasty food in the air fryer. You need to follow these instructions in the given order.

- Combine the chicken, cream cheese, chipotle, sauce, cumin, and chili powder in a large bowl. With salt and pepper, season.
- Place the tortillas on a secure microwave plate and cover them with a wet paper towel. Microwave for 30 seconds, or before more pliable and wet.
- Spread on one end of the tortilla about a quarter cup of filling, then scatter next to the filling a little cheddar and pepper jack. Tightly roll-up. Repeat with the filling and cheese.
- Place in the air fryer basket, seam side down, and cook for 7 minutes at 400 ° F.
- Serve with salsa, Pico de Gallo, and queso fresco with avocado cream.
- Mix the cilantro, avocado, sour cream, garlic and lime juice together in a food processor. With salt and pepper, season. Pour into a bowl and press directly over the top with plastic wrap, and refrigerate till ready to use.

3.18 Air Fryer Pizza

Preparation time

10 minutes

Servings

2 persons

Nutritional facts

345 calories

Ingredients

We have listed below the ingredients that would be required by you for cooking this healthy and tasty food in the air fryer:

- 2 (8-oz.) packages pizza dough
- 1 tablespoon extra-virgin olive oil, divided
- Freshly ground black pepper
- 1/2 (8-oz.) mozzarella ball, cut into Quarter" slices
- Basil leaves for serving
- One-third cup crushed tomatoes
- 1 clove garlic, minced
- A half teaspoon. oregano
- Kosher salt

Instructions

Given below are the detailed instructions for cooking this tasty food in the air fryer. You need to follow these instructions in the given order.

- Gently flatten the dough ball with your hands up to about 8" in diameter on a smooth, floured surface (or smaller than the basket of the air fryer). Repeat it with the second ball of dough. Brush both with olive oil and pass one to your air fryer's basket. Oil side up.
- Stir to mix crushed tomatoes, garlic, then oregano, and season with salt and pepper in a medium bowl. On the middle of the rolled-out pizza dough, spoon half the tomato mixture, then spread into an even layer, leaving 1/2" bare outer

crust.

- Apply half the slices of mozzarella to the pie. Air fry for 10 to 12 minutes at 400 ° F, or until the crust is golden and the cheese is melted.

- Using 2 sets of tongs, remove the first pizza from the air fryer basket and garnish it with basil leaves. Prepare and cook the second pizza, garnish and serve.

CHAPTER 4: Air Fryer Dinner Recipes

This chapter contains a collection of tasty lunch recipes that you can easily make in the air fryer.

4.1 Cajun Air Fryer Salmon

Preparation time

20 minutes

Servings

2 persons

Nutritional facts

327 calories

Ingredients

We have listed below the ingredients that would be required by you for cooking this healthy and tasty meal on your home air fryer:

- Original recipe yields 2 servings
- Ingredient Checklist
- Twelve ounces skin-on salmon fillets
- Cajun seasoning 1 teaspoon
- brown sugar
- cooking spray 1 tablespoon

Instructions

Given below are the detailed instructions for cooking this tasty meal on your air fryer. You need to follow these instructions in the given order.

- Heat the air fryer to three hundred ninety degrees F or 200 degrees C.
- Using a paper towel, dry the salmon fillets after rinsing them. Cooking spray can be sprayed on the fillets. In a small bowl, combine the Cajun spice as well as brown sugar. Using a fork, sift the ingredients onto a pan. Fillets' flesh sides should be pressed into the seasoning mix.
- Place salmon fillets skin-side down in the air fryer basket and spray with cooking spray. Spray the salmon with cooking spray once more.
- Cook for an additional ten minutes. Before eating, remove from the air fryer and set aside for 2 minutes to cool.

4.2 Air-Fryer Carrot Coffee Cake

Preparation time

50 minutes

Servings

6 persons

Nutritional facts

316 calories

Ingredients

We have listed below the ingredients that would be required by you for cooking this healthy and tasty meal on your home air fryer:

- One large egg, lightly beaten, room temperature
- A half-cup buttermilk
- A one third cup sugar plus 2 tablespoons sugar, divided
- 3 tablespoons canola oil
- 2 tablespoons dark brown sugar
- 1 teaspoon grated orange zest
- 1 teaspoon vanilla extract
- A two-third cup all-purpose flour
- A one-third cup white whole wheat flour
- 1 teaspoon baking powder
- two teaspoons pumpkin pie spice, divided
- A one-fourth teaspoon of baking soda
- A one-fourth teaspoon of salt
- One cup shredded carrots
- A quarter cup of dried cranberries
- A one-third cup chopped walnuts, toasted

Instructions

Given below are the detailed instructions for cooking this tasty meal on your air fryer. You need to follow these instructions in the given order.

- Heat air fryer to 350 degrees F.

- A 6-inch round baking pan should be greased and floured. Whisk together the orange zest, brown sugar, oil, egg, buttermilk, one-third cup sugar & vanilla in a big mixing bowl. Combine flours, baking soda, baking powder, one tsp pumpkin pie spice and salt in a separate dish. Gradually add the flour into the egg mixture. Combine the carrots as well as dried cranberries in a mixing bowl. Pour into the pan.

- Mix walnuts, the remaining 2 teaspoons cinnamon, and the remaining one tsp pumpkin spice in a shallow cup. Sprinkle uniformly on top of the batter. Place the pan in the basket of a broad air fryer gently.

- Cook for 35-40 minutes till a toothpick inserted in the middle comes out clean. If the top gets too black, cover it securely with foil. Cool for 10 minutes in the pan on a wire rack before withdrawing from the pan. It should be served warm.

4.3 Air-Fryer Greek Breadsticks

Preparation time

35 minutes

Servings

32 breadsticks

Nutritional facts

99 calories

Ingredients

We have listed below the ingredients that would be required by you for cooking this healthy and tasty meal on your home air fryer:

- A quarter cup artichoke hearts marinated and drained
- 2 tablespoons Greek olives, pitted
- One package (17.3 ounces) refrigerated puff pastry, thawed
- One carton (6-1/2 ounces) spreadable artichoke cream cheese and spinach
- 2 tablespoons Parmesan cheese, grated
- One large egg
- One tablespoon water
- two tsp. sesame seeds
- freeze tzatziki sauce, optional

Instructions

Given below are the detailed instructions for cooking this tasty meal on your air fryer. You need to follow these instructions in the given order.

- Heat air fryer to 325° F.
- In a food processor, mix artichokes and olives. Then cover and blend till finely chopped. On a lightly floured table, unfold 1 pastry sheet and spread half of the cream cheese on half of the pastry. Half of the artichoke mixture should be on top. Half of the Parmesan cheese should be sprinkled on top. Fold the simple half over the filling and softly press to close.

- Replace the leftover pastry, artichoke mixture, cream cheese and Parmesan cheese with the remaining ingredients. Brush tops with a mixture of egg plus water. Sesame seeds may be sprinkled on top. Every rectangle should be split into 16 3/4-inch-wide strips. Turn and Twist the strips a few times.

- Assemble breadsticks in the form of a single layer on a tray greased in the air-fryer basket in batches. Cook for 12 to 15 minutes, or till golden brown. If needed, serve with tzatziki sauce.

4.4 Air-Fryer Crumb-Topped Sole

Preparation time

20 minutes

Servings

4 persons

Nutritional facts

233 calories

Ingredients

We have listed below the ingredients that would be required by you for cooking this healthy and tasty meal on your home air fryer:

- Three tablespoons reduced-fat mayonnaise
- Three tablespoons grated Parmesan cheese, divided
- two teaspoons mustard seed
- A one-fourth teaspoon of pepper
- 4 sole fillets (6 ounces each)
- One cup soft bread crumbs
- One green onion, finely chopped
- A half teaspoon of ground mustard
- two teaspoons butter, melted
- Cooking spray

Instructions

Given below are the detailed instructions for cooking this tasty meal on your air fryer. You need to follow these instructions in the given order.

- Heat air fryer to 375° F.
- Mayonnaise, two tbsp cheese along with mustard seed and pepper are combined together and scattered over the tops of the fillets.
- Place the fish in an air-fryer basket in the form of a single layer on a greased plate. Cook for 3-5 minutes or until the fish flakes easily with just a fork.

- Meanwhile, mix bread crumbs, carrot, ground mustard, and the remaining 1 tbsp cheese in a small bowl; whisk in butter. Spritz topping in cooking spray and spoon over fillets, softly patting to stick. Cook for another 2-3 minutes until it's golden brown. Additional green onions may be sprinkled if needed.

4.5 Air Fried Radishes

Preparation time

25 minutes

Servings

6 persons

Nutritional facts

88 calories

Ingredients

We have listed below the ingredients that would be required by you for cooking this healthy and tasty meal on your home air fryer:

- Two and a quarter pounds radish, trimmed and quartered (about 6 cups)
- 3 tablespoons olive oil
- One tablespoon minced fresh oregano or 1 teaspoon dried oregano
- A one-fourth teaspoon of salt
- 1/8 teaspoon pepper

Instructions

Given below are the detailed instructions for cooking this tasty meal on your air fryer. You need to follow these instructions in the given order.

- Heat air fryer to 375°.
- Then mix radishes with the remaining ingredients.
- Then put radishes on a greased tray in the air-fryer basket.
- Cook it till it becomes crisp and tender for approximately twelve to fifteen minutes. Do not forget to stir occasionally.

4.6 Air-Fryer Eggplant Fries

Preparation time

25 minutes

Servings

6 persons

Nutritional facts

135 calories

Ingredients

We have listed below the ingredients that would be required by you for cooking this healthy and tasty meal on your home air fryer:

- Two large eggs
- A half-cup Parmesan cheese, grated
- A half-cup wheat germ, toasted
- One tsp. Italian seasoning
- 3/4 tsp. garlic salt
- One eggplant (about 1- ¼ pounds)
- Cooking oil for spray
- One cup warmed meatless pasta sauce

Instructions

Given below are the detailed instructions for cooking this tasty meal on your air fryer. You need to follow these instructions in the given order.

- Heat air fryer to 375° F.
- The eggs are to be whisked in a shallow bowl.
- Use a different bowl for mixing wheat germ, cheese and seasonings.
- The ends of the eggplant are to be trimmed. Then cut eggplant lengthwise into half-inch-thick slices.
- Next, cut slices into half-inch strips lengthwise. The eggplants are then dipped in eggs. Then they are coated with a cheese blend.

- Then assemble eggplants in the form of a single layer in batches on a greased tray in the air-fryer basket.

- Then spritz with cooking spray.

- It has to be cooked till golden brown for around four to five minutes. Then turn and spritz with cooking spray.

- Next, these have to be cooked till golden brown for approximately minutes.

- It is better to serve them with pasta sauce.

4.7 Air Fryer Salmon

Preparation time

15 minutes

Servings

2 persons

Nutritional facts

177calories

Ingredients

We have listed below the ingredients that would be required by you for cooking this healthy and tasty food in the air fryer:

- Freshly ground black pepper
- Two teaspoons. extra-virgin olive oil
- 2 tablespoons whole-grain mustard
- 1 tablespoon packed brown sugar
- 1 clove garlic, minced
- 2 (6-oz.) salmon fillets
- Kosher salt
- A half teaspoon. thyme leaves

Instructions

Given below are the detailed instructions for cooking this tasty food in the air fryer. You need to follow these instructions in the given order.

- Season salmon with salt and pepper all over. Whisk the sugar, oil, mustard, garlic and thyme together in a small dish. Spread atop the salmon.
- Arrange salmon in a basket of the air fryer. Set the air fryer to 400 degrees F. Now cook for 10 minutes.

4.8 Air Fryer Brussels Sprouts Chips

Preparation time

25 minutes

Servings

2-3 persons

Nutritional facts

205 calories

Ingredients

We have listed below the ingredients that would be required by you for cooking this healthy and tasty food in the air fryer:

- 2 tablespoons fresh Parmesan, grated, and more for garnish
- 1 teaspoon garlic powder
- 1/2 lb. Brussels sprouts, thinly sliced
- Kosher salt
- 1 tablespoon extra-virgin olive oil
- Grounded black pepper
- Caesar dressing
-

Instructions

Given below are the detailed instructions for cooking this tasty food in the air fryer. You need to follow these instructions in the given order.

- Toss the Brussels sprouts with garlic powder, oil and parmesan in a large bowl. Then season with salt & pepper. Arrange in the air fryer in an even layer.
- Bake for 8 minutes at 350°F, mix, and bake for 8 more minutes, until crispy and brown.
- For dipping, it can be garnished with more Parmesan. Then serve it with Caesar dressing.

4.9 Air Fryer Cheeseburger

Preparation time

30 minutes

Servings

4 persons

Nutritional facts

521 calories

Ingredients

We have listed below the ingredients that would be required by you for cooking this healthy and tasty food in the air fryer:

- 1 tablespoon low-sodium soy sauce
- Kosher salt
- Sliced tomatoes
- Thinly sliced red onion
- Freshly ground black pepper
- 4 slices American cheese
- 4 hamburger buns
- 1 lb. ground beef
- 2 cloves garlic, minced
- Mayonnaise
- Lettuce

Instructions

Given below are the detailed instructions for cooking this tasty food in the air fryer. You need to follow these instructions in the given order.

- Combine the soy sauce, beef and garlic in a large bowl. Shape and flatten into 4-inch circle 4 patties. With salt and pepper, season both sides.
- Put 2 patties in an air fryer and cook for four minutes per side, on average, at 375 °F. Remove and cover with a slice of cheese quickly. Repeat with 2 patties

left.

- Layer mayo on hamburger buns then finishes with tomatoes, lettuce, patties and onions.

4.10 Air Fryer Blooming Onion

Preparation time

45 minutes

Servings

4 persons

Nutritional facts

160 calories

Ingredients

We have listed below the ingredients that would be required by you for cooking this healthy and tasty food in the air fryer:

- 1 large yellow onion
- A half teaspoon. garlic powder
- 1/4 tsp dried oregano
- Kosher salt
- 3 large eggs
- 1 cup breadcrumbs
- Two teaspoons. paprika
- One tsp garlic powder
- One tsp onion powder
- One tsp kosher salt
- 3 tablespoons. extra-virgin olive oil
- 2/3 cup mayonnaise
- 2 tablespoons. ketchup
- One tsp horseradish
- A half teaspoon. Paprika

Instructions

Given below are the detailed instructions for cooking this tasty food in the air fryer.

You need to follow these instructions in the given order.

- Cut the onion stem off and arrange the onion on the flat side. Cut an inch from the root into 12 to 16 sections, being careful not to cut all the way. To remove petals, turn over and softly pull sections of onion out.

- Whisk the eggs and 1 tablespoon of water together in a shallow bowl. Whisk the breadcrumbs and spices together in another small bowl. Dip the onion into the egg wash, then dredge it in the breadcrumb paste, then cover it completely with a spoon. Sprinkle the onion with some oil.

- Place in the air fryer basket and cook at 375 ° F until the onion is tender, 20 to 25 minutes all the way through. Drizzle as needed with more oil.

- Meanwhile, make a sauce: stir together horseradish, mayonnaise, ketchup, paprika, garlic powder and dried oregano in a medium bowl, with salt, season.

- For dipping, serve the onion with sauce.

4.11 Air Fryer Potatoes

Preparation time

25 minutes

Servings

4 persons

Nutritional facts

160 calories

Ingredients

We have listed below the ingredients that would be required by you for cooking this healthy and tasty food in the air fryer:

- 1 pound baby potatoes, halved
- 1 tablespoon extra-virgin olive oil
- One tsp garlic powder
- One tsp Italian seasoning
- One tsp Cajun seasoning (optional)
- Kosher salt
- Freshly ground black pepper
- Lemon wedge, for serving
- Freshly chopped parsley for garnish

Instructions

Given below are the detailed instructions for cooking this tasty food in the air fryer. You need to follow these instructions in the given order.

- Toss potatoes with Cajun seasoning, Italian seasoning, oil and garlic powder in a large bowl. With salt and pepper, season.
- Place the potatoes in an air fryer basket and cook for 10 minutes at 400 ° F. Shake the basket and stir the potatoes and cook for another 8 to 10 minutes, until the potatoes are golden and soft.

- Squeeze the lemon juice over the fried potatoes and garnish before serving with parsley.

4.12 Air Fryer Chicken Breast

Preparation time

30 minutes

Servings

2 persons

Nutritional facts

257 calories

Ingredients

We have listed below the ingredients that would be required by you for cooking this healthy and tasty food in the air fryer:

- One large egg, beaten
- 1/4 cup all-purpose flour
- 3/4 cup panko bread crumbs
- One-third cup freshly grated Parmesan
- Two teaspoons. lemon zest
- 1 tsp dried oregano
- A half teaspoon. cayenne pepper
- Kosher salt
- Freshly ground black pepper
- Two boneless skinless chicken breasts

Instructions

Given below are the detailed instructions for cooking this tasty food in the air fryer. You need to follow these instructions in the given order.

- Place in two separate shallow bowls the eggs and starch. Combine the oregano, panko, parmesan, lemon zest and cayenne in the third shallow bowl. With salt and pepper, season.
- Dip the chicken into the flour, then the eggs, and then the panko paste, pressing to cover, one at a time.

- Put in the air-fryer basket and cook for 10 minutes at 375 °F. Flip the chicken and cook for another five minutes until the chicken is golden and cooked through.

4.13 Air Fryer Pork Chops

Preparation time

20 minutes

Servings

4 persons

Nutritional facts

488 calories

Ingredients

We have listed below the ingredients that would be required by you for cooking this healthy and tasty food in the air fryer:

- 4 boneless pork chops
- 1 tsp. kosher salt
- 1 tsp. paprika
- 1 tsp. garlic powder
- 1 tsp. onion powder
- 2 tablespoons. extra-virgin olive oil
- Half cup freshly grated Parmesan
- A half teaspoon. freshly ground black pepper

Instructions

Given below are the detailed instructions for cooking this tasty food in the air fryer. You need to follow these instructions in the given order.

- Pat-dry pork chops with paper towels. Cover the two sides with oil. Combine the parmesan and spices in a medium bowl. Coat the pork chops with Parmesan paste on both sides.
- Place pork chops in an air-fryer basket and cook for 9 minutes at 375 ° F, flipping midway through.

4.14 Air Fryer Rotisserie Chicken

Preparation time

1 hour 10 minutes

Servings

6 persons

Nutritional facts

260 calories

Ingredients

We have listed below the ingredients that would be required by you for cooking this healthy and tasty food in the air fryer:

- 1 (3-lb) chicken, cut into 8 pieces
- Two teaspoons.
- 2 tablespoons dried oregano
- Two teaspoons garlic powder
- Two teaspoons onion powder
- 1 tsp. smoked paprika
- Kosher salt
- Freshly ground black pepper
- 1 tablespoon dried thyme
- 1/4 tsp cayenne

Instructions

Given below are the detailed instructions for cooking this tasty food in the air fryer. You need to follow these instructions in the given order.

- Season the chicken pieces with salt and pepper all over. Whisk the herbs and spices together in a medium bowl, then brush the spice mix all over the chicken bits.
- Insert dark pieces of meat into the air fryer basket and cook 10 minutes at 350 ° F. Then flip and cook ten minutes more. Repeat for chicken breasts; however,

reduce the time per side to eight minutes. To ensure the chicken is cooked through, using a meat thermometer, each piece should reach 165 ° F.

4.15 Best-Ever Mozzarella Sticks

Preparation time

2 hours 25 minutes

Servings

6 persons

Nutritional facts

230 calories

Ingredients

We have listed below the ingredients that would be required by you for cooking this healthy and tasty food in the air fryer:

- 6 mozzarella sticks
- 2 large eggs, well-beaten
- 3 tablespoons all-purpose flour
- One cup panko bread crumbs
- Kosher salt
- Freshly cracked black pepper
- Warm marinara, for serving

Instructions

Given below are the detailed instructions for cooking this tasty food in the air fryer. You need to follow these instructions in the given order.

- Freeze sticks of mozzarella until completely frozen, at least 2 hours.
- Establish a breading station after 3 hours: Put panko, eggs, and flour in three different shallow bowls. With salt and pepper, season the panko generously.
- Frozen mozzarella sticks are covered in flour, then soaked in eggs, then panko, back in the egg, finally back in the panko.
- Arrange in the air fryer's basket frozen sticks of breaded mozzarella in an even layer. Cook for 6 minutes at 400 ° F, or until the exterior is golden and crisp and melted in the middle.

- It can be served with warm marinara sauce.

4.16 Air Fryer Garlic Herb Turkey Breast

Preparation time

1 hour

Servings

6 persons

Nutritional facts

286 calories

Ingredients

We have listed below the ingredients that would be required by you for cooking this healthy and tasty food in the air fryer:

- 2 pounds turkey breast, skin on
- Kosher salt
- Freshly ground black pepper
- 1 tsp freshly chopped thyme
- 4 tablespoons. butter, melted
- 3 cloves garlic, minced
- 1 tsp freshly chopped rosemary

Instructions

Given below are the detailed instructions for cooking this tasty food in the air fryer. You need to follow these instructions in the given order.

Dry the turkey breast and season with salt and pepper on both sides.

- Combine the thyme, melted butter, garlic and rosemary in a shallow bowl. Brush the butter all over the breast of the turkey.
- Put in the air fryer basket, skin side up. Now cook for 40 minutes at 375 ° F or until the internal temperature exceeds 160 °F, turning halfway through.
- Allow 5 minutes to rest before slicing.

4.17 Air Fryer Sriracha-Honey Chicken Wings

Preparation time

40 minutes

Servings

2 persons

Nutritional facts

197 calories

Ingredients

We have listed below the ingredients that would be required by you for cooking this healthy and tasty food in the air fryer:

- Two tablespoons sriracha sauce
- One and a half tablespoon soy sauce
- 1 tablespoon butter
- juice of 1/2 lime
- 1 pound chicken wings, tips removed, and wings cut into individual drummettes and flats
- A quarter cup of honey
- cilantro, chives, or scallions for garnish

Instructions

Given below are the detailed instructions for cooking this tasty food in the air fryer. You need to follow these instructions in the given order.

- The air fryer is preheated to 360 degrees F. To make sure the wings are sufficiently browned, put the chicken wings into the air fryer basket and cook for thirty minutes, turning the chicken around every 7 minutes with tongs.
- Insert the sauce ingredients into a small saucepan as the wings are frying, and bring to a boil for about three minutes.
- Toss them in a bowl with the sauce when the wings are cooked until thoroughly covered. Then sprinkle with the garnish. Serve immediately.

4.18 Garlic Herb Turkey Breast Deep Fryer

Preparation time

5 hours 8 minutes

Servings

3 persons

Nutritional facts

179 calories

Ingredients

We have listed below the ingredients that would be required by you for cooking this healthy and tasty food in the air fryer:

- Guacamole
- 2 teaspoons cumin
- fresh finely chopped cilantro to taste (about One-third cup)
- sea salt & pepper to taste
- 8 tablespoons fine almond flour
- One egg
- One egg white
- One third cup almond flour
- 3 medium ripe avocados
- juice from 1 lime
- One-third cup chopped onion
- Substitute: unflavored protein powder or protein baking powder; coconut flour; tapioca or arrowroot powder
- 90g (One and a half cups gluten-free panko
- Substitute: regular panko; wheat breadcrumbs
- spray olive oil

Instructions

Given below are the detailed instructions for cooking this tasty food in the air fryer. You need to follow these instructions in the given order.

- In a bowl, combine and mash the guacamole ingredients without the almond flour. Add in the almond flour until you have the perfect spice, until the guacamole is dense, like brownie batter. To make it thick, add additional tablespoons of almond flour to the batter as needed. As this can leave the guacamole wet and loose, be careful not to apply too much lime juice. Set the bowl to harden for 1-2 hours in the freezer until it has hardened.

- Line with parchment paper or nonstick foil the baking sheet. Use a spoon to scoop the guacamole out and shape a ball with your hands, about the size of a ping pong ball, and put it on the baking tray. Repeat with the leftover guacamole VERY easily. Use nonstick foil to protect the tray and place it in the freezer for at least 4 hours or overnight.

- Set air fryer to the 390F (199C).

- Eggs are beaten together in a bowl.

- You MUST work hard, and you will definitely have to do this in batches. To make them get 'sticky,' gently brush a guacamole ball in olive oil, then dip it in almond flour, egg mixture, panko crumbs. Repeat ONLY until you have enough guacamole balls to fill the basket of the air fryer, so placing the remainder of the balls back in the freezer (without coating).

- Place the coated balls in the basket of the air fryer, spray with a little olive oil and cook for 6 to 8 minutes or until golden brown on the outside. Keep them out of the air fryer if the balls start cracking. Allow them to cool slightly before treating because as they cool, they become firmer.

4.19 Air Fried German Pancakes

Preparation time

13 minutes

Servings

2persons

Nutritional facts

139 calories

Ingredients

We have listed below the ingredients that would be required by you for cooking this healthy and tasty food in the air fryer:

- Three whole eggs
- Substitutes: coconut milk; reduced-fat milk; 2% whole milk
- Pinch of salt
- Two heaping tablespoons of unsweetened applesauce (optional yet recommended to replace the need for added oil or butter)
- Fresh berries
- Swerve confectioner's sugar
- Raw unsweetened cacao nibs (for crunch and antioxidants)
- 1 cup whole wheat flour
- Substitutes: oat flour
- 1 cup almond milk
- Greek yogurt
- Maple syrup (optional)

Instructions

Given below are the detailed instructions for cooking this tasty food in the air fryer. You need to follow these instructions in the given order.

- Set the air-fryer to 390F/199C. As it heats, place the cast iron tray or ramekin within the air fryer.

- Add all the batter components to a blender and mix until creamy. Also, add teaspoons of milk along with applesauce to thin it out if the batter appears to be too thick.

- Spray with nonstick baking spray on a cast iron tray or ramekin. Then pour the batter into a serving.

- It is to be air fried for 6 to 8 minutes. If the top comes out sort of hard to handle, do not worry. This is the advantage of using the air fryer-it gives a good firm exterior coating/edges to the pancake that softens as it cools.

- To keep it fresh every morning, put the leftover batter in an airtight jar in the fridge.

- Garnish and rejoice.

Conclusion

Air fried food has recently become popular, much as microwave ovens did in the 1980s. Famous fast foods like French fries, chicken wings, and fish sticks are said to be lower in fat when air fried. You may be scratching your head, uncertain what air-fried food is all about. An air fryer is a device that resembles a rice cooker or a standard fryer in appearance. It works, though, by circulating hot air all over the food to make the outside crisp and crunchy. A Maillard reaction occurs, in which the food's amino acids react with the reducing sugars, resulting in succulent, flavorful food. Instead of being fully immersed in oil, air-frying helps you to obtain a comparable outcome with only one tablespoon of oil. Air fryers help you shed weight by reducing the amount of fat you consume. Foods prepared by deep-frying have a higher fat content than foods prepared by other processes. According to certain producers, food fried in a traditional manner contains about thirty-three percent fatter than food prepared in an oven. They say that air fryers will reduce the fat content of fried food by up to 75%. How is this accomplished? Air fryers, on the other hand, only use one tablespoon of oil compared to three cups in a normal fryer. This may be really good news for people who are at risk of heart failure and other coronary artery diseases. Air fryers can aid in weight loss. Dietary fat provides half as many calories as other macronutrients, including carbohydrates and protein, with 9 calories per gram. It logically follows that air-fried food aids in the reduction of calories and weight loss. When it comes to deep-frying vs. air-frying, air-frying still wins. Fried food, in general, can contain dangerous compounds like acrylamide, which is typically found in high carb foods fried at extreme temps. According to certain reports, an air fryer may help to reduce this to a degree of up to 90%. Certain compounds (aldehydes, heterocyclic amines, and polycyclic aromatic hydrocarbons, for example) are still present, so air frying can reduce but not remove these hazards. Two of the best foods for air frying are chicken and potatoes. A crispy layer and succulent core can be found with some easy seasoning on the chicken. Air fryers may also be used to turn vegetables that children hate into crispy snacks that they can enjoy. Sweet potato fries are a great example of something tasty that can be made in an air fryer in a relatively short time. A BPA-free plastic model can reduce health risks even further and give you peace of mind while frying food using air fryers.

Printed in Great Britain
by Amazon

64656866R00066